The Tragedy of Mr No Balance

by Kwo Victor Elame Musinga

edited with an introduction by Roselyne M. Jua

Langaa **Research & Publishing CIG**
Mankon, Bamenda

Publisher:

Langaa RPCIG
(*Langaa* Research & Publishing Common Initiative Group)
P.O. Box 902 Mankon
Bamenda
North West Province
Cameroon
Langaagrp@gmail.com
www.langaapublisher.com

Distributed outside N. America by African Books Collective
orders@africanbookscollective.com
www.africanbookscollective.com

Distributed in N. America by Michigan State University Press
msupress@msu.edu
www.msupress.msu.edu

ISBN:9956-558-98-2

DISCLAIMER

All views expressed in this publication are those of the author and do not necessarily reflect the views of Langaa RPCIG.

Contents

Introduction

The plays of Victor Elame Musinga are many and diverse but little known. A man of small stature with an effacing temperament, this creative spirit is liable to be overlooked in any gathering. In conversation he tells you that he started writing poetry and seems to have simply stumbled onto playwriting. With well over thirty plays to his credit one would imagine him a household name. Yet this is not the case. The recent outcry for more literary publications by Anglophones, while justifiable, nevertheless failed to take into account Musinga's stock of plays. Little known, read or applauded, Musinga has continued to write, to stage productions and has more recently taken up interest in television with his drama group. What has accounted for this relative obscurity? Several reasons immediately raise their ugly heads: The absence of veritable publishing houses which has reduced most writers to desk-top publishing is clearly a case in point. Could the deteriorating standards of a now quiescent reading public explain this situation? Would it be a sour note to raise the point that seemingly Anglophone dramatists have actively sought to teach and/or produce drama written solely by fellow academicians almost exclusively including themselves? Whatever the justification, in depicting corruption and greed and how they transform a once rational being into an irrational nincompoop, Musinga's *The Tragedy of Mr. No Balance* suggests that there must always be a balance in society and situates his work within the parameters of the post colony. This has accounted for *No-Balance's* seminal quality even given its disappearance from print for the lessons it teaches are as eloquent today as they were in 1964 when it was first written. This present edition which in redressing the situation again projects it to the lime-light participates literally and metaphorically in establishing that *balance*. A brief summary of the play may not only be helpful but needful at this point.[1]

Musinga's *The Tragedy of Mr. No-Balance* written in 1964 depicts the downfall of Zacharias Kongmelina No-Balance, a young Chief Clerk of Vemsarbatreborp Corporation. Not content with his salary he is desirous of all the good things money can buy. He will get rich quick by any means possible regardless of several warnings from his friend, Ernest and even his own conscience, Voice, as presented in the very first scene of the play. The drama unwinds when No-Balance begins to realize that even the get-rich-quick scheme he has coalesced will not suffice and he must consequently modulate his approach. He has failed to take cognizance of the other players he has tried to dupe, and even a rudimentary summation of all his expected income should prove to him that just like the first, the second scheme will not render him rich quickly. Bih, the simpleton he recruited because *he* seemed the candidate most likely to acquiesce to all his demands ironically catapults his unmasking in this dramatization of

---

[1] We have appended Michael Etherton's comments addressed to the playwright when the play was first staged. We hope that these comments will be of some help to production directors in particular.

greed and victimization. Bih's report to the Police instigates the downward spiral in the unravelling and undoing of No-Balance's career. But, No-Balance is to everyone's dismay acquitted since the Prosecution is unable to tender burden of proof. However, No-Balance is immediately re-arrested and charged with attempting to corrupt the forces of law and order. The evidence available is overwhelming; he suffers a reversal of fortune and is sentenced to "seven years imprisonment with very hard labour." No-Balance must face the consequences of his actions and at a time when he should find solace with Mbarama he is alone and solitary. She deserts him and rightly so; he had also spurned her for the salaried Maggie, also younger and more beautiful than Mbarama. Unmasked and convicted he can only regret the fact that he had refused to listen to his own counsel and friend and stayed honest in all his dealings.

Chris Dunton opines of *The Tragedy of Mr. No-Balance*: "There is a disjunction between the satirical energies that are fore grounded through the larger part of Musinga's play and the emphasis on the constructive role of State agencies that emerges in the latter part of the play and that dominate its closing moments" and muses further "that the jury is still out."[2] While the validity of Dunton's initial claim need not be transfused given the content of the play, in retrospect the verdict is in; the die has been cast and what appears as a fissure is really the author attempting to distance himself from the inevitable conclusion one must accomplish given the events that unfold. For Musinga's musings as far as State machinery is concerned is as true today as it was for Cameroon in the early 1960's when the East and the West came together under the umbrella of the Federal Republic of Cameroon. The issue of corruption, whether in the private sphere or in the public domain is as germane today as it was in 1964 when the play was first written and subsequently presented to the public for the first time. That even the name of the country has since undergone various permutations, progressing to United Republic and ultimately back to La Republique du Cameroon without popular consultation in this yet emerging nation caught in the throes of a repressive regime emphasizes the need for the *balance* that had been suggested in the appellation "Federal" or even "United" since they demonstrated the merging of two entities thereby successfully foregrounding what has come to be called "the Anglophone problem."[3]

There is *no balance* and the double pun is intended for unlike Mr. No-Balance's assertion in this play aptly named after him, it is not "life" but death that has come abundantly. That is the interpretation one must give to incarceration in this play, an

---

[2] Chris Dunton makes this assertion in a forthcoming publication entitled "Life in Abundance is Come: Victor Musinga's *The Tragedy of Mr. No-Balance*." Jua, Roselyne M., Bate Besong, Hilarious N. Ambe & Neba Ayun'wi Neba eds. *Emerging Perspectives 1*. Forthcoming publication

[3] Explanations as well as definitions of "the Anglophone problem" have been postulated by scholars across the disciplines. See for example Hilarious N. Ambe, "The Anglophone-Francophone Marriage and Anglophone Dramatic Compositions in the Cameroon Republic" (2004) and Piet Konings & Francis Nyamnjoh, Negotiating an Anglophone Identity (2003).

analogy that Bole Butake and Bate Besong would continue to extend and portray in *Lake God*, *And Palm Wine Will Flow*, *Beasts of No Nation* and *Requiem for the Last Kaiser* to name a few plays in the tradition. The rift is thus to be apprehended as part and parcel of the constructing metaphor yoking interrelated dissonance.

The play's enduring quality speaks to the seminal nature of the protagonist, Z. K. No-Balance, as well as the topicality and referentiality of its subject matter in today's Cameroon even forty years since it was first written and produced on stage as Musinga interrogates the complexity of Cameroon's political landscape. Depicting the transition from victimizer to victim, Musinga illustrates drama that pits man against a timeless nemesis – greed. Therefore, the play can be interpreted as political satire; the affiliation between art, in this case, drama and politics has been accentuated by notable scholars like Wole Soyinka () and M. K. (1975), and even history records that the great Persian Kings used art for political gain. So whereas politicians have been known to use art, particularly the theatre as a propaganda weapon, they have cried foul when this same medium has been used by non-politicians to reflect some of the ills of the society. It becomes impossible to state as categorically as Benjamin Bennett (1992) that any discourse on hermeneutics can be abstracted from performance. This is justified in the court scene where the first verdict provokes a gasp of unbelief from the court audience and spectators and the second a sigh of relief and exhalation. Judge Snaps' final judgment reveals the possibility for a world where justice exists and where people do obtain their just rewards where the first suggests the contrary to its imputation in the scales no balance and willy nilly broaches the subject of how difficult it is sometimes to exercise justice within an inept judicial system.

The Ancients like Socrates, Euripides and Sophocles as well as critics like Plato and Aristotle established the intimate relationship between the playwright and his environment and society and this is no less true of Musinga and his Drama Group.[4] Set in immediate post independent West Cameroon when shops like United Trading Company (UTC) and PRINTANIA landmarks of colonialism were still operational, a time when interpreters were essential for any communication between the white colonial master and the colonized African and were thus privileged by virtue of their *perceived* literacy,[5] **No-Balance** also exhibits in a paradoxical manner, nostalgia for a past where Rule of Law was operational. Redress was swift and just; corruption was not the

---

[4] The Musinga Drama Group, the pioneer theatre troupe, was founded in November 1973 by an ardent, budding Cameroonian Dramatist, Victor Elame Musinga, with 15 actors and actresses. Its maiden performance for the appreciation of the Cameroonian public was *The Trials of Ngowo*. The troupe featured prominently at the National Festival of Arts and Culture in 1974 at which it won first place and the subsequent national tour this instigated fermented its acclaim as it proceeded *inter alia* on a cultural renaissance and to nudge awake a comatose society.

[5] No-Balance it is clear as events unfold in the play is semi-literate; he obfuscates the English Language at will to serve his personal interest.

order of the day as displayed in the competent and swift actions of Justice Snaps and the Police Officers exhibiting traits to a public which can only dream that working in tandem the forces of law and order can protect the underprivileged. In retrospect it becomes a salient comment on the present condition of bribery and corruption in all the arms of government; the Executive, the Legislative and the Judicial. The Police/gendarmes commonly propagate lawlessness and incivility as evinced on highways where motor vehicle infractions are countenanced upon the culprits' presentation of 500FCFA or even less; they have been satirically nicknamed "Mange Mille." Some members of the judiciary have been known to demand huge sums of money from plaintiffs and defendants to help sway the opinion of the Court. High ranking members of government have also been known to embezzle State funds with impunity. But even Civil Servants have used the bottle-necks of the Service for personal aggrandizement, demanding monetary compensation before files concerned with financial matters can be treated. Clearly, it can be perceived as a comment on the *rot* permeating all of the Cameroonian society to use Marcellus' declaration of Denmark in *Hamlet* (I. iv 90) or the "shitocracy" which Bate Besong depicts in *Beasts of No Nation* and in this light Musinga becomes very much the seer in the Platonian sense. In other words, Cameroonians, especially civil servants, who are interested only in self-serving appointments to higher office or live by what Jean-Francois Bayart has appropriately labelled "la politique du ventre"[6] are themselves accountable, at least in part, for the malaise in which the country finds itself. Notice the speed with which No-Balance transfers affection from Mbarama his "tomato" just departed to take care of a sick Aunt to Maggie, supposedly Mbarama's Aunt and they both refer to each other as husband and wife in Scene 7 and how quickly No-Balance will modify the relationship to that of sister-in-law as he tries to wiggle out of the case of having bribed a police office.

Ask theatre-goers in Anglophone Cameroon who Victor Elame Musinga is and the response you get is -- The author of *Mr. No-Balance*. One remarks the popularity of the play and a denial almost to acknowledge the tragic quality inscribed in its title. This dissonance between the audience and the action on stage emerges because "the people who attend his plays immediately recognize traits, attributes and impulses they have witnessed in the real world" (Bjornson 256) or what Eyoh has simply called audience identification. The playwright is not the "detached observer who contemplates it from a position of social superiority" as he seeks to create a "common humanity in the midst of social change" (Etherton), but a proponent of forum theatre as Boal suggests, except that in this case that interaction is only implied in the audience response to the action on stage. Musinga will tell you that on any given day he listens closely to conversations around him and works these into that night's performance. Speech patterns and

---

[6] Loosely translated this reads "the politics of the stomach." See Bayart, Jean-François. "Foreword." In *L'Etat en Afrique: La Politique du Ventre*. Paris: Fayard, 1996.

language expressions are very close to daily utterance. In subordinating the reality of lives lived, Musinga's emphasis on performance in the celebration of playwriting evokes an egalitarian world in his drama if we agree with Boal that theatre is seductive, "a way of making people feel more alive, because to participate they have to think; they have to measure the consequences of what they are proposing" (Unwin).

Musinga proposes that one can see or appreciate the comic or satirical even in everyday experiences; even personal experiences become matter for public theatre or entertainment. I refer here to three particular occurrences in his life. Playing football as a child with a limp, he was inevitably given the nickname No-Balance. Returning home from Nigeria, he would drop job applications everywhere only to meet with rejection. And finally, as all young handsome men are wont, he would fall in love. The young lady was called Bih and Musinga believed at the time that Bih was her surname. Only later would he discover that children from the North-West Province do actually bear their own names. Art took ascendancy. Bih would become the catalyst for No-Balance's undoing in more ways than one; in real life as in drama. My discussions with the playwright during the editorial process highlighted Musinga's conception of Bih as a woman. This knowledge we have transmitted to the audience/reader only. Psychoanalysts and feminists will have a field day with this, and rightly so. A woman postures as a man, retains her female name and refuses to divulge her real identity. Only the audience if they are quick enough are privileged to apprehend in her *aside* that they are dealing with a female character and likely even to overlook this for Musinga seems bent on erasing boundaries as he creates and explores new dynamic frontiers in Anglophone Cameroon dramaturgy.

Of all Anglophone Cameroonian dramatists, Musinga renders a more dynamic exploration of the female character in his plays like Njema in *Njema*, Ngowo in *The Trials of Ngowo*, Fende in *The Challenge of Fende* and Madam Magrano in *Madam Magrano* due probably to the fact that his plays are all issue based; that is, he takes a specific problem within the society and in the manner of forum theatre or community theatre tries to suggest a remedy for that particular problem. A cursory look at popular Anglophone Cameroonian plays tends to confirm the oft held opinion that Bole Butake as well as Bate Besong needs to be singled out of the pack for their female characters. Whereas female characters appear in Besong's plays, they do so as abstractions bearing no names and therefore no individuality, no personality and no character; they are simply lumped together and called "Woman" as in *Requiem for the Last Kaiser*. Butake seems more equivocal in his portrayal and relation to women. His oft quoted remarks in an interview to Onjeme serve as a reference point for this assertion:

> Inasmuch as women are concerned, I think that I have looked around in our modern society and I find that women have practically thrown in the towel into […] the boxing rings and abandoned the fight. […] There is so much that is going on in our society in terms of economic development, political awareness, and educational and social development […] and women have

tended to accept to be left out[….] As far as I am concerned, the men folk have been such a disappointment that I have completely lost faith in them. I am hoping that perhaps the women can now take the battle stick and maybe try to do something about straightening up the injustices that are reigning in our society. Perhaps that is one reason why I tend to give women a very specific or outstanding place in my works. (Interview 1992)

Butake's disappointment in modern man's role in contemporary social global politics and economics is borne out in popular plays like *Lake God*, *And Palm wine Will Flow*, and *The Survivors* which portray failed male politics and intimate that only women, agents of social peace, can restore order in the land. But interestingly, what Butake may on the one hand concede to women, he immediately retracts with the other. Whereas strong individual female characters abound such as Yensi in *Lake God*, Mboysi in *The Survivors* and Kwengong in *And Palm wine Will Flow*, these women are restricted to performance within rural communities and group action. Kwengong, if and when she must act alone, must also put on the disguise of "Earth Goddess" in order to act. Obviously her actions are the actions of "Earth Goddess," with the implication that the supernatural world manipulates the actions of the real world which by itself is unable to act. Butake's relegation of women to social groupings within specific rural communities paradoxically intimates that women have no role within the urban set-up, undermines any achievement by women in modern day Cameroon and speaks to the paternalistic attitude that women continue to encounter in their daily lives. In other words, it is not women who have abandoned the fight for social justice but men who refuse to engage women in revolutionary discourse apart from that assigned them traditionally even given man's recognition of evolving times in Ngujoh's upbraid to Old One's claim in *The Survivors* that in the old days men negotiated only with other men:

Never mind your times, Old One. *Those days were ancient days. Today, women are the key to power.* Even the door with seven locks on it can be unlocked by a woman. (65) (my emphasis)

But Ngujoh's recognition of feminine power does not stop here. He immediately affirms that in those "days [*they*] used reason" (65), implies that women do not employ reason and insinuates that feminine guile and lust, to put it mildly, are now the weapons of destruction and/or coercion.

The woman is not one dimensional in the works of Musinga. Musinga's Bih assumes male disguise with ironic and satiric consequences as she confronts the inequalities of the patriarchy and bests a man. The effectiveness of Bih's mask lies in the fact that she voluntarily reveals her womanhood to the audience in Scene 2 in an aside but deliberately withholds this knowledge from the rest of the cast of characters on stage. The question this provokes is who is using who here? For while No-Balance recognizes that he is squeezing money unduly from Bih, it is clear to the audience that the illiterate sluggish Bih perceived as decrepit is also exploiting No-Balance.

Bih's assumption of a masculine role is comparable to No-Balance's pretension to the posts of Manager of Vemsarbatreborp Corporation and husband of Mbarama. Bih's intelligence has continuously been underestimated by No-Balance since the former could *read* the latter perfectly as noted in the first utterance in Scene 1: "I see your eyes and actions want me to give you or to show you the dash." And even No-Balance had in Scene 4 noted during the interview that Bih could understand "equivocal statements" when Tm and Jack could not. That by Scene 5, Bih who has barely put in a days work is already asking for "bicycle allowance" should put No-Balance on his guard. Not doing so engenders his undoing. Moreover, Bih's disguise also interrogates the subject of comparable worth which as Carolyn H. Magid suggests has implications for radical social transformation (125). In this light, Bih's sexual transformation decries inequality in the work place; it is only as a man that she can obtain employment. Refusing her state of deprivation and/or inertia and then redefining her own agenda, Bih literally and metaphorically blasts her way from the periphery to the centre as postulated by feminist critics like hooks.[7]

Maggie, no ordinary woman, excels as an undercover cop; a fact even her male superiors acknowledge as they rely solely on her to bring-in No-Balance. So, whereas No-Balance believes in Scenes 1 and 7 that he can like the Cameroonian male take advantage of a distressed woman, Bih and Maggie have the last laugh and bring back order to the unwedded garden. One of the dilemmas that Musinga poses in the process is the insinuation that justice, law and order can seemingly only be obtained through entrapment and that is what constitutes part of the tragedy of *Mr. No-Balance*.

Mbarama, No-Balance's live-in girlfriend and "temptress" seemingly catapults him on his greedy unscrupulous search for undeserved wealth with her insistence that No-Balance provide her with the comforts of a rich life such as a car and house servant. She fulfils the woman's traditional role as nurturer providing food for his flatulence but also metaphorically feeds his ego as in Scene 3 when she refers to his intelligence. But, the revelation during the court scene that No-Balance had in her absence begun to court Maggie propels Mbarama to self-assertion and redemption. She tells No-Balance off, leaves him to his fate and refuses to succumb to her supportive role.

No-Balance's solitary cry as he is marched off to prison which signals his recognition that he has been outsmarted, raises questions of victim hood and juxtaposes survival with victimization. Who is victimizing who in this play? Having previously suffered victimization, Bih empowers herself and now becomes a survivor but in a convoluted sense also a victimizer and victim. Bih set out to entrap No-Balance but the judgment rendered falls far short of victory for her/him. She is clearly also trapped in her restricting male gear and cognizant of the fact that men are uncomfortable performing domestic duties, like sweeping and cleaning, the preserve of women, she must act clumsily like a man. On the other hand, a reversal prevails since No-Balance, who launched the victimization of others himself becomes a victim, albeit

---

[7] See hooks, bell. "Feminism: A Movement to End Sexist Oppression."

of circumstances as he puts it. In perceiving only the substantial growth of his own personal bank account to the detriment of the other party and also as in this case how efficacy in the workplace becomes jeopardized by his actions No-Balance exemplifies a society corrupt to the core. No-Balance confiscates not only another's dream but usurps individual liberties.

Also worth noting is the fact that at its first staging the part of Judge Snaps was acted by a woman -- Ama Mundi. In all therefore, we have not three but four women who play consequential roles at each stage in No-Balance's life. Clearly, substantive female characters imbue the work of no other Anglophone Cameroonian playwright as they have with Musinga apart from maybe in more recent years the plays of Anne Tanyi-Tang.[8] Musinga's historic situation of a woman's potential, recognizes her centrality to the politico-socio-economic discourse be it in the eradication of corruption, the flight against social ills like prostitution or approbation of our evolving traditional values. In retrospect, Musinga advocated female leadership long before it became fashionable or politically correct.

In 1991 a bellicose Jean-Stephen Biatcha erstwhile government spy and Director of Sports and Cultural Activities at the University stalked out of a Butake production of Bate Besong's *Beasts of No Nation* (by the University of Yaounde Theatre Troupe) which depicts the stench and corruption characterizing mythical Ednuoay to write his now infamous report:

> It is a clear political pamphlet directed at the regime in power that is held responsible for the economic crisis through corruption, favouritism and capital flight to foreign banks. The author holds the thesis that Francophones in power are responsible for the economic crisis because they are producers of waste matter, embezzlers of public funds. [...]The author equally affirms, and this is the central thesis (philosophy) of the play that Anglophones of Cameroon are marginalized and confined to undignified roles like that of "carriers of excrement."[...] At the end of the performance, the playwright took to the stage to publicly declare that the future of Cameroon is uncertain and that chaos can set in at any time. (Translated Shadrach A. Ambanasom 223)[9]

The similarities engaged here in *Beasts of No Nation* were at best allusive and needed a foray into an understanding of metaphor and metonymy to say the least. This perceived

---

[8] See for example the following plays by Musinga: *Fantastic Madam Ida*, *The Challenge of Fende*, *Lily*, *Madam Magrano*, *Njema* etc all devoted to espousing crucial issues of the day from a more englobing gendered perspective.

[9] Jean-Stephen Biatcha's confidential report entitled "A la haute attention de Monsieur le Chancelier d'Université de Yaoundé" was published in *Challenge Hebdo* No. 0045 of Oct. 23-Nov. 6 1991, a French Language weekly.

attack on the State earned for Besong a two day incarceration in the CENER premises and subsequent victimization on the part of State agencies as the playwright holds.[10] Government reaction here is characteristic of a paranoid totalitarian mind set and Besong's *Beasts* illustrated the bestiality inherent in fictional Ednuoay (read Yaounde backwards). But clearly Biatcha and the government had missed the whole point of Besong's play which was not principally aimed at criticizing a corrupt government but whose aim was as Ngugi Wa O`Thiongo has stated elsewhere to "free the manacled spirit and energy of our people so we can build a new country, and sing a new song." Imagine then the consternation and political backlash a production of Musinga's *No-Balance* would provoke in the present uneasy climate rash with accusations of public embezzlement of billions rendering some crooks richer than the State.[11] No-Balance refers in Scene 7 to the vices creeping into the young State but forgets that he is himself contributing to this state of affairs. So even though the primary function of the artist is not that of seer Musinga's *No-Balance* effectively reflects the rage of bribery and corruption in the country. However, unlike as obtains for No-Balance the public awaits judgment for all those accused of embezzlement for the watch word mentioned by Jack in Scene 4 is patriotic. The immediate question is, will life now imitate art? The die has in other words been cast and the sigh of relief No-Balance's incarceration provokes demonstrates how the artist's imagination liberates from an oppressive reality. The tragedy is, however, that in a world absent of morality, there is no consciousness of good and evil and there can be no balance.

Works Cited

Ambanasom, Shadrach A. "Pedagogy of the Deprived. A Study of the Plays of Victor Epie Ngome, Bole Butake and Bate Besong." *Epasa Moto.* 1 3 1996 218-227.

Ambe, Hilarious N. The Anglophone-Francophone Marriage and Anglophone Dramatic Compositions in the Cameroon Republic. Peter H. Marsden and Geoffrey V. Davis eds. *Towards a Transcultural Future: Literature and Human Rights in a 'Post'-Colonial World.* Amsterdam, New York: Rodopi, 2004 71-80.

Barba, Eugenio and Judy Barba. The Deep Order Called Turbulence: The Three Faces of Dramaturgy. *The Drama Review.* 44 4 2000, 56-66.

Bayart, Jean-François: "Foreword." In *L'Etat en Afrique: La Politique du Ventre.* Paris: Fayard, 1996.

Bennet, Benjamin. "Performance and the Exposure of Hermeneutics." *Theatre Journal.*

---

[10] See Bate Besong's interview with Pierre Fandio where he speaks of humiliating demotions suffered, financial ruin and the bann placed on his works in *ALA Bulletin.*

[11] These millionaires and the indecent figures siphoned from the common man's sweat in Cameroon Bank and other state agencies have been published in both the Anglophone and Francophone dailies such as *Le Jeune Observateur,* August 2007, *The Post* and *Le Messager,* 9 January 2008

44 4 431-447.

Besong, Bate. *Beasts of No Nation*. Limbe: Pressbook, 1998.

Biatcha, Jean-Stephen. "A la haute attention de Monsieur le Chancelier d'Université de Yaoundé." *Challenge Hebdo* No. 0045 Oct. 23-Nov. 6 1991.

Bjornson, Richard. *The African Quest for Freedom and Identity: Cameroonian Writing and the National Experience*. Bloomington, Indianapolis: Indiana University P, 1991.

Boal, Augusto. *Legislative Theatre: Using performance to make politics*. Translated Adrian Jackson, London and New York: Routledge, 1998.

Butake, Bole. *Lake God*. In Bole Butake *Lake God and Other Plays*. Yaoundé: Editions Cle, 1999, 5-58.

---. *The Survivors*. *Lake God and Other Plays*. 59-85.

---. *And Palm-Wine Will Flow*. *Lake God and Other Plays*. 87-142.

Danesi, Marcel & Paul Perron. *Analyzing Cultures*. Bloomington and Indiana: Indiana University Press, 1999.

Etherton, Michael. "Some Production comments" addressed to Mr. Musinga. Unpublished. (See Appendix 1).

Fandio, Pierre. "Anglophone Cameroon Literature at the Cross Roads: Pierre Fandio in Conversation with Cameroonian Writer, Bate Besong." *ALA Bulletin*. 30 2 Fall 2004/Winter 2005, 90-104.

hooks, bell. "Feminism: A Movement to End Sexist Oppression." In *Feminist Theory: from margin to centre*. 17-31.

Konings, Piet and Francis Nyamnjoh. *Negotiating an Anglophone Identity*. Leiden and Boston: Brill, 2003.

Magid, Carolyn H. "Does Comparable Worth Have Radical Potential?" Patrice DiQuinzio and Iris Marion Young ed. *Feminist Ethics & Social Policy*. Bloomington and Indianapolis: Indiana University Press, 1997, 125-142.

Musinga, Victor Elame. *The Tragedy of Mr. No-Balance*. Unpublished.

M. K. Introduction. Political Theatre Issue. *The Drama Review*. 19 2 3 (June 1975).

Shakespeare, William. *Hamlet, Prince of Denmark*. Sylvan Barnet ed. *The Complete Signet Classic Shakespeare*. New York: Harcourt Brace Jovanovich, Inc. 1963, 917 – 961.

Unwin, Sophie. "Resurgence." http://resurgtence.gn.apc.org/ (March 31, 2002), "Force for Change," interview.

Cast of Characters

Vaa, Manager of Vemsarbatreborp Corporation
No-Balance, Chief clerk of Vemsarbatreborp Corporation
Ernest, Friend to No-Balance
Mbarama, Concubine to No-Balance
Miss Muke, Typist at Vemsarbatreborp Corporation
Wawah, Clerk in Vemsarbatreborp Corporation
Tim, First Applicant
Jack, Second Applicant
Bih, Third Applicant
Cyclist
Edie, A.S P. (Security)
Beagles Constable
Asongbu, Constable/Postman
Maggie Lady Officer, Upper Secret Branch of the Police.
Snaps, High Court Judge
Pat, Prosecutor
Law, Court Clerk
Zaacs, First witness for the accused
Voice, Conscience of No-Balance
(The play was first produced under the title *Mr. No-Balance Tastes Bribery*)

Scene I

It is 2p.m. **Mr. No-Balance** *returns home after the day's hard work, completely worn-out and hungry. Seeing that the dining-table is not yet set, he becomes enraged.* **Mbarama**, *his girlfriend, who in the course of preparing a meal injured herself, has in anger given up and is dozing in a chair.* **No-Balance** *wakes her up as soon as he comes in.*

No-Balance: Now Madam, tell me why these irregularities in this house?

Mbarama: What has caused these irregularities?

No-Balance: What! Talking to me like that? I'm hungry, my lunch is not ready and you've the hell of a mind to lie comfortably in a chair bought by me!

Mbarama *(Jerking herself up and forcing her finger forward into his face)*: Look at my finger, wet with my blood. What negotiations have you with the gods to cause my losing a pint of my blood by your not employing a cook in spite of countless pleadings? Speak! Answer me, mister! *(weeps)*.

No-Balance *(cools down)*: Mbarama, I do not see that as sufficient reason for you not prepare me, at least, something to keep up my fast deflating sack. Moreover, you know for certain that my salary at present doesn't suffice to our fullest -- I mean, to have a car, a servant and some other pleasures. *(Smiles and pats her on the back)* Darling, just take it easy.

Mbarama: But remember, you promised giving me all comforts needed by a lady of my calibre.

No-Balance: A wooer's language. All the same, *(pats his stomach)* fill my sack and I'll give you all the comforts, as much as comforts could be given to a lady.

Mbarama: Now, you have for the second time in plain language promised to ... *(she is interrupted by a knock on the door)*.

No-Balance: Come in, please. It's all right. My sack is just collapsing *(A young man, decently dressed, comes in. He is **Ernest**)*

Ernest: Boy. O boy!

No-Balance: Wonderful! Ernest! You're the last person I ever expected meeting again, Ten years out of sight has played some changes on you. Without mincing words, you've amassed a fortune. *(**Ernest** fixes his eyes on **Mbarama** with contempt as she walks out)*.

1

Ernest: Who's that painted Jezebel? Hope she's not your wife!

No-Balance (*confused*): Ah! There goes Miss Mbarama of (*he calls out to her*) O.K. B about our meal.

Ernest: I'll not partake of the meal. I've only come to keep you in the know, tha my wife has put to birth a baby boy; would you like to come round and drink to its health?

No-Balance: Unless I eat! (*pats his stomach*) My sack is so empty it cannot stand uprigh for much longer. Again, transport this way isn't as sure as…

Ernest: What transport are you complaining of? Sorry to keep you in the dark I'm now the proud owner of a Mercedes-Benz car. It's just two hundred yards from here. (**No-Balance** *gapes in amazement.*)

(*Mbarama enters, sets the table, and goes out again.*)

No-Balance: Permit me do some justice here, please. (*He eats hungrily*) Now, Ernest let us come back to our good old days and talk matters over nicely. It' *your* secret I wish you to disclose to me. First, how did you come abou your fortune; second, what help can you render my securing mine withir the week?

Ernest (*laughs*): You may not believe me if I tell you. However, it's this simple: b honest, be fair in your dealings with men, and success will be at you door.

No-Balance (*frowns*): Are you saying of me that I don't practice honesty or what are you up to?

Ernest: No-Balance, be not downcast. You asked for my formula. That's the formula I used to achieve my success in life. I apply it to my day-to-da activity, and nothing fails me. You could formulate yours, but you mus be honest and …

No-Balance (*cuts in vehemently*): Keep quiet and die with your formula. No-Balance need none of your formulae.

Ernest: I see you're in the firm grip of jealousy; in the highest greed fo overnight riches.

No-Balance: Be quiet, I say. I'll have none of your fooleries any longer.

(Silence. Mbarama re-enters.)

Ernest: Mbarama, I have a word of advice for you and your money minded husband before I take my leave. Honesty of purpose in dealing with men has many advantages over deceit; it is an easier mode in dispatching business, it inspires men with greater confidence and also places you in the path of having a car, a servant and a decent home.

(Ernest goes out dejectedly)

No-Balance: Mbarama, I tell you, you'll soon hear that Ernest has gone mad before the balance of this month.

Mbarama: Isn't he your friend? I saw him to be a deceiver and a rogue too. Anyway, let's drink to his having left.

No-Balance: Get us a bottle of whisky to stimulate us. I want to devise something.

*(She clears the table and goes away. He sits down to some serious thinking. A few minutes later, it becomes apparent that he has hit upon a plan as he smiles and dances about. **Mbarama** re-enters with the whisky).*

Mbarama: Are you welcoming this drink by dancing, or what's in the air?

No-Balance *(kisses her)*: Darling, life in abundance is come! You'll any hour from now start getting all the comforts you need.

Mbarama: What's it? Sip your whisky while you school me to it.

No-Balance: You know for all the world that I'm the Chief Clerk of our Corporation. But for the Manager, I'm second to none. At present, we've no office boy and this slows down the working of the office. Now, I'll importune the Manager to allow me advertise for the post of an office boy. And I'm dead sure with unemployment in prevalence here, 1001 will apply. I'll then ask each applicant to give me some money, by the by, to attend a test. He who gives me the highest amount, gets the job, irrespective of his performance in the test. *(sips his wine)* And this, done and finished with, *(sips his wine)* there'll be money, money all the way! *(Mbarama sips her drink, inhales deeply and nods her head)* So, you give to my masterful plan a

3

deep breath of relief; a nod of your head and a sip of your wine; Why not crown all with a kiss?

Mbarama: Take it easy. Is this not what they call Bri-be-ry?

No-Balance (*his eyes goggling*): So, up to this age, you don't yet understand the meaning of the word bribery! Bribery is taking money from a person, not persons, with an eye to securing him a job. But in this case, there are several persons, and a test, too.

Mbarama: Will the amount they'll give you suffice to get us a car, a servant and...

No-Balance: Definitely, and even more. My salary is 50,000 francs per month. What other activity have I to do with money apart from seeing about our pleasures? My children will have to fight it for themselves.

Mbarama (*hesitates then kisses him*): Approved! Approved! No more turning back. We can now relax and get ready for the task at hand. (*She goes out. Then **Voice** is heard, a deep rolling sound coming from within **No-Balance**. The latter looks frightened*)

Voice: You've a desire and that I appreciate. But note that desire is tremendous force and must be directed in the right channel or misfortune will be the ultimate result.
(***No-Balance** gazes at the empty space with fright, then, shrugs his shoulders and goes out deep in thought*).

*At **Mr. No-Balance's** Office the following morning; we see a cross-section of No-Balance's Office; **Wawah** is at his desk and Miss Muke, the typist, is busy typing. Shortly thereafter **No-Balance** walks in. He's in a gay and happy mood. He approaches **Wawah**.*

No-Balance: Mr. Wawah, it appears you've nothing doing this morning?

Wawah: Exactly so, sir. I cleared my tray yesterday.

No-Balance: Hard working chap. And I'm afraid; I've nothing for you today. (*pauses*) Anyway, if you won't mind it, I grant you this day, a holiday. You can now go home and be about your private business.

Wawah: I'm very grateful, sir.

No-Balance: Don't mention it.

(***Wawah*** *goes out while **Miss Muke** continues to type*)

No-Balance: A minute, Miss Muke. (*She stops typing*) If my memory serves me right, you did some time ago ask for permission to pay a short visit to your sick mother?

Muke: That I did, sir.

No-Balance: Was it granted you?

Muke: It wasn't, sir.

No-Balance: I'm sorry. But do you still long to pay her a visit?

Muke: Certainly, sir.

No-Balance: All right. I grant you three days off duty as from now. Hope that serves you well? (*Silence, then she responds shyly*)

Muke: It's a pity sir. I'm so badly off now that I've to defer it until I'm well off again.

No-Balance: Don't worry. (*Gives her 1000 francs note*) Have this for your transport and other expenses. Extend my best wishes to your mother. (*She starts to roll off the paper from the machine but No-Balance stops her*) Don't take off the

5

paper, I'll continue the work.

Muke: Thank you very much indeed, sir.

No-Balance: Don't mention it. I'm only doing my duty. (*Muke goes out*)

Voice (*Intruding once more*) Who-so-ever is delighted in Self-lonesomeness, i always at the mercy of the merciless gods.

No-Balance (*in an enraged mood*): Anyone may consider it very absurd of me, but it's step which has been masterfully calculated. (*He feigns anger and sets abou littering the office with waste papers, scattering books on the Manager's table an doing everything to annoy anyone keen on tidiness. He sits down very unhappily t work. Moments later, **Vaa** enters, looks around the office and frowns*)

Vaa: Why's the office so untidy? Is there nobody to tidy it up? By the way where're Miss Muke and Mr. Wawah? (*No-Balance in disdain looks him u and down, sighs, and continues with his work*) O.K! that's all one.

(**Vaa** *sits down. Silence. Then* **No-Balance** *moves up to* **Vaa's** *table, his hand in his pockets*)

No-Balance: Mr. Vaa, you're the Manager of this Corporation, and I, the Chief Clerl Do you dispute this? (*Vaa who is concentrating on a sheet of paper on his tab simply shakes his head in affirmation without looking away from the paper*) Now if you value my presence in this Corporation, nay, this office, as much a I do yours, let us from this moment, employ an office boy; and you'll ge the best of my services. If this is not done, I'll tender my resignatio before the close of the day's work. (*He moves back to his seat, lights a cigaret and exhales the smoke. Silence*)

Vaa: I hope you had no nightmare last night, Mr. No-Balance? What right have you on earth not to talk of heaven, to address me, your Manage with your hands in your pockets? Put those thoughts from your minc The devil is getting at you.

No-Balance: Whatever the devil intends of me, our securing an office boy wi counteract it all. Anyway, I hope it's nothing bad; for though a devil, believe not all devils are bad. (*Short silence*)

Vaa: Where did you say Miss Muke and Mr. Wawah have gone to?

6

No-Balance: Mr. Wawah, according to his medical report, is suffering from anti-parasympathetic activity. So, the doctor has given him some days off-duty. As for Miss Muke, when she got a telephone call this morning informing her of her mother's death I gave her some days off-duty; she ran out wildly and even forgot taking the paper off the machine.

Vaa: Oh-sorry for Mr. Wawah's illness and Miss Muke's bereavement. What a day of illness and bereavement! To crown it all, I'm now off on a two weeks tour of all our agencies. You know all the workings of the office. To facilitate your work, advertise for an office boy of good qualities (*No-Balance's face brightens up*) Place him on a fair salary. I hope to have nothing but good reports on my return. Bye for now.
(*Vaa goes out, and there is silence*)

No-Balance: Knowledge, no matter the source, makes a man. But after all, does knowledge not come from God? So, God approves of my master device. Wonderful! Wonderful!

Voice (*cuts in*): Damnation! This is the turning point of your life. Amend! Amend!

(*No-Balance goes away. Shortly, he returns with a board on which he writes up the following notice*)

VACANCY

A smart boy is wanted in this office for the post of an office boy.
Age: Must be between 16 and 18 years of age.
Qualification: Should have the ability of understanding equivocal statements irrespective of educational background.
Conduct: Must be submissive under all normal and abnormal circumstances.
Tribe: No tribal but racial discrimination.
Salary: Wonderfully, unbelievably attractive.

Apply in person, today!!!!!

Z.K. No-Balance
Prospective Manager

(*No-Balance displays the notice outside the office. Almost immediately Tim presents himself as an applicant for the post. He is neatly dressed.*)

Tim: Good morning, sir. I've come to present myself as a candidate for the post of an office boy as advertised outside.

No-Balance: What's your name? Where are you from? Who're your parents? And how far and fast can you reason?

Tim: Tim is my name. I come from Motombolombo and my parents are farmers. I have the First School Leaving Certificate with three credits. I can reason as far and fast as my intellect can go.

No-Balance: That's just what I want. Now, all you have to do is to call at my house tomorrow at 10.00 a.m. As soon as it's 10.10 a.m. don't come again, understood? As to my house, just call near the biggest tap in town and ask for Meno's quarters, and you'll get me with the least difficulty. O.K?

Tim: Quite O.K., sir. (*Tim starts to leave*)

No-Balance (*pretending to recollect*): Aha! Boy, remember to throw water up when you come to my house tomorrow.

Tim: It's all right, sir.

(*Tim exits. There is silence, Then **Jack**, shabbily dressed, enters without knocking and leaves the door wide open behind him.*)

Jack: I've come so that ..,

No-Balance: Shut the door and behave well.

(***Jack** shuts the door, turns, pulls up a seat and sits down haughtily to the bewilderment of **No-Balance**.*)

Jack: Yes. I want to be an office boy here as stated on the board, can I?

No-Balance: What's your name? What's..?

Jack: Hold on. I'm no machine. Jack is my name,

No-Balance: Your tribe, your parents, how far and fast can you reason?

Jack: Why care to know my tribe? Am I of a different race? However, Bangwi is my tribe. Untold tycoon, my father's designation. My reasoning faculty, as far as to

8

Jericho and at a speed of unbelievable kilometres per second.

No-Balance: What you have to do is come to my house tomorrow at 10: 15 a.m. And note, as soon as it's 10: 25 a.m. don't come again. Clear?

Jack: Was it dark at first? I hope you stay at Meno's quarters?

No-Balance: That's right. Again, don't forget to oil my lips tomorrow when you come.

Jack: Ha! Luckily, my father also deals in assorted oils. Your lips will be painted with the seven colours of the rainbow tomorrow. (*he goes out, but returns immediately*) This is the prospective office boy saying bye-bye to the prospective manager.

(***Jack** smiles and exits. Enter **Bih** unkempt and dull in appearance.*)

Bih: Good morning, sah. My name is Bih. For two years now, I have not worked. Everywhere I go, I heard big people like you, ask me for dash. I had no sense about this, but now, I know it. God said, ask and you go get; me too now say ask for dash for oil or grease and I prepare for it. No more talk. I have some small dash here for you sah. I see by your eyes and actions that you want me to give you or to show you the dash. (*He brings out a stack of bank notes from his pocket and places it on the table*)

No-Balance: Put the money back in your pocket. (***Bih** does so*) A genius is a genius. You've the petroleum of ingenuity anointed on you. How much money have you there?

Bih: I get here 10,000 francs.

(***No-Balance** writes it down*)

No-Balance: All the same, call at my house tomorrow at 10.30 a.m. I need to have some talk with you. And remember, this work has a never-heard of salary; so try to do more and displace any other person.

Bih (*about to run out*): I fit run back to the house for more.

No-Balance (*stops him*): No, no, no. It's almost time now to close up the office. Just call tomorrow as promised; do your level best, and leave the rest to God and me.

Bih: Sah, try harder for me, sah. (As ***Bih** exits she says in an aside to the audience.* No be only my money but dis my man pikin clothes whey go get me this job! *Silence.*)

No-Balance: I've worked overtime today and immediately paid myself for it. Therefore, my money is well deserved. Am I not honesty itself?

Voice: O man! you're not honest. Remember, honesty of purpose in dealing with men is above this money.

No-Balance (*boldly*): Look here, you invisible coward of a spirit: if you have nothing doing, transform yourself into human form; and I'll consider you for my house-boy. I'll have money all along

(***No-Balance*** *goes off.*)

It is morning and we are *back at **Mr. No-Balance's*** house. ***No-Balance*** *has three appointments to keep. He comes in not yet fully dressed brushing his teeth with a "chewing stick." He looks at his watch, stops brushing his teeth, and calls out to **Mbarama**.*

No-Balance: Mbarama, darling! Tomato!

Mbarama (*Walking in*): Yes, what's the matter?

No-Balance: Why put on such a long face today? Please cheer up, for it's today that we'll reap the fruits of our labour. Now, those applicants will come in with some gifts for us. You stay behind the house or in the room. I'll direct them to you as they come in. Get whatever they give you, write the amount or nature of gifts against their names on this paper, (*handing her a sheet of paper of a very conspicuous colour*). It is from the gift that I'll determine my future office boy. Lest I forget, Bih looks a sure employee. Nevertheless, let's watch the intensity of the competition. It's now 10.00 a.m. and here comes the first one, Tim.

    (***Mbarama*** *hurries out to take up her place as **Tim** knocks and enters with a container of water, which he places in a corner of the room unnoticed by **No-Balance**.*)

Tim: Good morning, sir. I've come as promised.

No-Balance: You're right on time.

Tim: Sir, you know that punctuality is the soul of business.

No-Balance (*waiving it*): Now, follow my wife and show her your kindness.

    (*As Tim goes out, he takes the container of water still unnoticed by **No-Balance**. There is a scream from the next room and **Mbarama** enters in a fury, completely soaked.*)

No-Balance: What is this that you're sweating so much when we're now on business?

Mbarama (*slaps **No-Balance** on the cheek*): Is this the comfort or plan you have for me? You negotiate with people to come and bathe me in my dress in your house?

    (*Tim enters with the container, now empty.*)

No-Balance (*confused*): Tim, is this how you exhibit your ability or your kindness? Do you know that I can now charge you with assault on my wife?

Tim (*apologetically*): My lips cannot express the sorrow in my heart; do not punish me for the mistake and I'll show much diligence at work.

No-Balance (*looking at his watch*): Oh! Get out. I'm expecting an august guest. And look here, you may turn up for the test tomorrow if you wish, but you've already baptized yourself with an incredible degree of failure. Thank you (*Tim goes out. No-Balance turns to Mbarama*) Darling, take it easy and resume your place for here comes another.

(*Jack enters. He is carrying a bag over his shoulders in which are bottles of oils. He has his shirt carelessly thrown on his body.*)

Jack (*panting*): Sir, what's the time? Am … Am … Am I late? I was doing some laundry when I immediately recollected my appointment of oiling your lips. Then, I jumped out and made for here at Apollo-like speed; lest I be late and forfeit that post with an …

No-Balance: Unbelievably attractive salary. Cool down my boy. There's no need worrying. You're just some odd seconds ahead of time

Jack (*looking for a seat*): Really!! I thought I was late. Weh! God's really with me. This job, naturally, is mine.

No-Balance: Now, see my wife there in the room and show her your kindness.

Jack (*he is just going out, but recollects and returns*): But what of the oils? I've here all types of oils needed by a prospective manager. Here you have: (*produces the bottles of oils one by one and places each on the table as he names them*) palm oil, groundnut oil, shampoo oil, rubbing oil, engine oil and...

No-Balance (*cutting in angrily*): O.K. O.K. O Lord, I'm doomed to fresh disappointment.

Jack (*anxiously*): Which of the oils do you wish me to start oiling your lips with?

No-Balance: Just see my wife.

Jack (*confused*): I thought I saw your wife go out as I came in, or should I commence the oiling on her? No, she was wet; you want me ascertain for you she's all right now. Never mind, I'll do it.

No-Balance: See her, and then away you go.

(*Jack goes out and returns shortly exclaiming in praise of Mbarama*)

Jack: Wonderful! Wonderful! Unearthly! Smashing! Dashing! Radiating! Exquisite! Divine! Unbelievable! Forever! With and never without! Never without! Never! Never! Never!

(*He is completely lost in thought about Mbarama's beauty so much so that he roams the lounge as if invoking the gods while* **No-Balance** *looks on in surprise*)

No-Balance: What is it? Are you hypnotized?

Jack: It's your wife! I've seen her and believe me, you've the world round, a unique sense for the beauty. No wonder you want all types of oils in decorating your lips with. Are you wedding tomorrow? Can I become your best boy? Lest I forget, she has taken the oils from me. Well sir, get an artist to assist you in the decoration and think over the questions you're to ask tomorrow. Bye-bye sir. (*As he goes off he meets Bih on the way in*) Friend, are you for Mr. No-Balance's house, yes or no?

Bih: Yes. (*Jack looks angry, which frightens* **Bih** *who alters his answer*). No. (*Jack smiles again*).

Jack: I thought you're also for the appointment. But how far are you going?

Bih: (*cowardly, points in the opposite direction*) Just there. .

Jack: Safe journey.

(**Bih** *lingers around until Jack disappears out of sight, then he swerves and makes for No-Balance's house. Knocks and enters*).

Bih: Good morning, sah.

No-Balance (*stands up and welcomes him*): Aha! Good boy. Just see my wife, then go home and prepare very hard for tomorrow's test. (**Bih** *goes out; some minutes later,* **Mbarama** *enter smiling*).

Mbarama: Tomato, I've come to render my account about the applicants, as

13

follows:

> Tim -- though he has book knowledge, he doesn't behave well. So
> instead of prosecuting him for bad behaviour, make him forfeit the job
> Jack -- what an arrogant fellow who cares little for anything! Som
> bottles of oils, do you lack oils? Forget about him, even if he get
> through the test. Bih -- God bless him Money! Money! Money! He get
> the job even under abnormal circumstances, He…

No-Balance (*cuts in*):   Abnormal circumstances is one of the conditions I outlined i
the advertisement. So, I'm covered.

Mbarama: He presented us with 16,000 francs.

No-Balance: And he showed me 10,000 francs in the office yesterday. (*Mbaram*
caresses No-Balance)

Mbarama: My husband, it's now agreed and confirmed, you have money an
intelligence, too. If men don't place you high in their minds just don'
worry; for, I today declare you the conquest of mine. Now, what next?

No-Balance (*proudly*):   You know better. I think a car first, to drive ourselves to th
four corners of pleasure and safety. (*They go off*)

*It is Monday morning. At Mr. No-Balance's office, all are present for the test but Bih. There's growing impatience, when **Bih** strolls in sluggishly*

Bih: I'm sorry to be late. I were getting up late and I tries too

Jack (*cutting in with a laugh*):   Is this a candidate for this test? He cannot make a simple, correct sentence! You're done for my...

No-Balance: Shut up. It's none of your business. Your test consists of mental work, only. Now, when I ask anyone a question, the answer must be given in a twinkle of an eye. Now, number one Question is for Tim 0x0x0x0x0x0-0-0-0-0x10?

Tim: 0

No-Balance: Yes. Now number two question is for Jack. 30 - 30? (***Jack** stands up and looks steadily at Mr. No-Balance. There is silence for a few seconds*) Well, it's more than time allowed. You're unable to answer it. You have zero there.

Jack (*protesting*):   Did you twinkle your eyes to indicate that I should answer? I have been watching you that you twinkle your eyes before I answer, but you didn't. After all, didn't t you instruct to answer in a twinkle of an eye? You've instead failed in officiating accordingly.
I'll do it myself. (*He sits down, blinks, and answers*) The answer is zero or in simple mathematical terms naught.

No-Balance (*releases a heavy breath*): Number three question is for Bih. 0x0?

Bih (*racks his brain*): Em … Em … Em …

No-Balance (*cutting in*): I forgot that you're a stammerer. You say naught?

Bih: Yes. Naught. (***Tim** and **Jack** look at each other*)

No-Balance: This is the last set and it will be difficult.

Jack: Only remember my bottles of oils and repay me reasonably.

No-Balance: Who is the President of Ka…?

Jack (*cutting In with a jump*):   President Ahidjo!

No-Balance (*enraged*):   Was it your turn or did I call you up? More so, did I ask for the name of the President of Cameroon?

Jack: You shaped your lips to pronounce the name Cameroon, and that jarred me up. I, again, being a patriot of my country, couldn't sit down to hear a dunce rack his brain over such a simple question. This, however, exhibits in me two qualities: one, my ability to answer in a twinkle of an eye; two, my knowledge of understanding equivocal statements in no time.

No-Balance: Sit down there. You have zero here.

Jack: What are you talking about? I'm going away. This is no test. There's some foul play here. (*He stands up as if to go away*)

No-Balance: Now, Tim and Bih, as prospective Manager of this corporation, where is my likely residence when I own a car?

Jack (*cutting in*): In jail! And I'll drive you into the prison yard in your car! (***Jack** goes out. There is a short silence*)

No-Balance: Mister Tim, now that you are two of you, I'd like to know something of you. Which do you prefer: to go to jail or forfeit this job?

Tim: All sounds the same, Sir. But why am I to go to jail?

No-Balance (*hushing him to be silent*):   Do you remember the disgrace you gave my wife in my own house? I have a good mind now to phone for the police. Should I do so? (*He pretends to be looking for the telephone when **Tim** prevents him and pleads*)

Tim: No, sir. I'll go away right now. I'm sorry for what I did.

No-Balance: You asked for a punishment and that's it. No job for you. Thank you.

Tim (*as he starts to leave*): O God! O God, forbid the ghost. Why, was I born to suffer? So, I'm doomed for life. Must I then turn to dishonesty? Nevertheless, every dog has its own day. Today is Bih's. (***Tim** exits*)

No-Balance (*looks at Bih, happily*):   Bih, have a handshake on your success. They say, today is your day. Little do they know of your power of

	understanding equivocal statements? It's wonderful! Now, let's come to business. You'll be paid as an office boy 4,500 francs per month. I see you like it. I'll make you all right at all times. Your duties will be: to be here at 8: 00 a. m. prompt, sweep the office, and tidy up the tables. You will also answer calls by the Manager. Don't for all the world go astray; or it is going to be your fault. And remember this: whenever you are in doubt about something or in difficulties, signal me by clicking your fingers, and I'll come to your aid. Understood?

Bih: Yes sah.

No-Balance: You may now set yourself about your work, while I go out for a few minutes. I mean, you tidy up the place.

(*He goes out while **Bih** gets busy seemingly arranging some books on No-Balance's table. Clumsily, he knocks over the bottle of ink spilling the contents over the papers on the table and soiling his fingers as well. Consequently, any paper or furniture he touches becomes soiled. Then, he gets a rope, places the chairs and tables together and tries to tie them up, when **No-Balance** enters whistling.*)

No-Balance: What! Finger-marks on the table, wall, and even chairs! What's cooking here boy? Again, what are you doing with the chairs and tables? Is this how we are to get on?

Bih: But master ask me to tie up the things and place.

No-Balance (*remarks in disgust*): Illiterates are no good! (*He helps in tidying up the office. **Vaa** enters*)

Vaa: Hello! I've come back sooner than I expected. I can see you're as busy as a bee. How busy you must have been during my absence!

No-Balance (*perspiring with fright*): Uneasy lies the head that wears the crown.

Vaa (*frowning as his eyes fall on Bih*): Who's this sluggard? I hope he's not our new office boy?

No-Balance: Just be patient and listen to a verbatim account of the working of the office during your absence. (*Turns to Bih*) All right boy, you can close up for the day and remember to be here tomorrow at 8: 00 a. m. prompt.

*As Bih exits **Vaa's** eyes trail him with dissatisfaction. **No-Balance** moves up a*

17

chair to Vaa's table and they confer.

Vaa: Before we talk any serious matter, will you please give me an account of the recruitment which favoured this sluggard. Remember the quality of the boy -- he should be smart.

No-Balance *(composing himself)*: It all went thus: as I set out the advertisement, fifty applicants put in an appearance in thirty minutes. Happily you're acquainted with the prevalence of unemployment here. Well, I eliminated some by retaining the most neatly dressed ones. Only three were retained and this Bih was among the three and the neatest also. Satisfied for that moment, I at once gave the three said boys a mental test. And believe you me; the problems were so difficult that... I *(pretends to search for the non-existing question paper, but **Vaa** waves it aside)* sorry I've destroyed it ...they would take a well-read scholar time to answer. But to my surprise, Bih answered them with such ease that I was forced to employ him and make him start work then and there, lest I do him and this corporation injustice. Though slow in his movements, he's like a tadpole when dropped into fresh water. It takes some days to master the forces around. There's one important point to be mentioned, a thief broke into their house and made away with his certificates. So, we need not bother our- selves much about his certificates. After all, the advertisement reads: a smart boy and not a smart looking boy. All the same; see him in action tomorrow.

Vaa: Well and good. I will accept your story for now. I'm tired and feeling drowsy and need a long rest. I will hear more tomorrow and see more of your office boy before I take any decision.

.

> *Vaa exits. **No-Balance** exhales, visibly relieved and muses aloud.*

No-Balance: Man! I almost slipped. Now, to my house I go, to have my darling's unique comfort. (*Exit **No-Balance***)

Scene V

It is now morning, and the street is crowded with people busily hurrying to their offices and others to their businesses. Pedestrians, motor-cyclists, and bicycle riders are seen hurrying along in various directions. No-Balance is conspicuous in the crowd. Joggled by a fast moving pedestrian, he is enraged and this sets him haranguing aloud. He can move through the audience to the stage.

No-Balance: Oh me! When can I own a car and save myself from these brutal treatments from curs of low degree? By the way No-Balance, a Peugeot car costs 900,000 francs, and my salary for the last three months plus the presents given me by the office boy cannot purchase me one, not even on hire-purchase. How then am I going to obtain my wish? Mbarama must be satisfied at all cost. I made a mistake to have advertised for an office boy. (*He is so deep in thought that a cyclist after jingling his bell for him to give way brushes him and almost knocks him down*).

Cyclist: My friend, are you mad? If you're looking for your death, it's not from me that you'll get it. Scallywag! (***No-Balance*** *moves on quite unperturbed and continues his musings out loud*)

No-Balance: Nevertheless, the brain is there. As from tomorrow morning, I will feign sickness, and then look for somebody to officiate during my sick period, Now, in the course of his officiating, I will ask him to bribe – no, to present me with a heavy sum of money in order that I speak to the Manager about our getting an Assistant Chief Clerk. This proposal will definitely be approved of, and *he*, lucky devil, will be the one I will recommend. Then, I too, with my money in hand and some in the bank will be able to go up to the Peugeot sales company and issue a cheque for a car in my name. (*Smiles*) This must be done three days from now if I am to impress my only tomato darling, Mbarama.

(***No-Balance*** *looks at his watch realizes he is late and moves speedily towards the stage which is now his office.* ***Vaa*** *has already arrived there, on time. No-Balance is late. Bih has not yet come in and the office is untidy.* ***Vaa*** *becomes impatient.* ***No-Balance*** *comes in, does not find Bih and now begins to look worried. Shortly thereafter,* ***Bih*** *enters panting and adjusting his pair of shorts.*)

Bih: Good morning sahs! I sorry to enter late. I slept and stand only at 7.30 a.m. this morning. Again, my house is far away from the office. Sah, I beg for bicycle allowance.

Vaa: Are you complaining or explaining the cause of your coming late? By the way, have you been asked a question? Just, set yourself about your work. I will see about your sluggishness. (*Bih starts sweeping the floor without watering it; this raises* a cloud of dust which further irritates *Vaa* all the more). Boy... did you at all learn the rules of hygiene? What do you do before you sweep? (*Bih racks his brain in search of an*

answer. Unable to find one he clicks his finger as a signal to No-Balance to come to his aid. No-Balance gets a bottle of water and sprinkles some on the floor. Still, *Bih* does not catch on). Well Mr. No-Balance, there is your clever office boy! It is mere commonsense.

No-Balance: Cleverness is no commonsense, and commonsense you know well is naturally not common.

Vaa: Agreed, for the moment.

(*They sit down to work while **Bih** waits outside.*)

No-Balance: Excuse me, sir. Won't it be better to re-arrange the office, now we have an office boy? (*On pronouncing the words "office boy" **Bih** answers and comes in*)

Bih: Yes sah!

Vaa: Yes boy, what can I do for you?

Bih: I hear "office boy."

No-Balance (*cutting in*): I am sorry. His parents complained to me of his suffering from hallucination. I am sure it's got over him now...

Bih (*rebuffs him*): No sah! I am not suffer from halla ... hallo ...lo ...

Vaa: This is too much!!! (*Bih exits. **Vaa** turns to No-Balance.*) Now, Mr. No-Balance, I've heard and seen enough of Bih's so-called "cleverness" and his being a victim to hallucination. I no longer wish to hear any more explanations in his defence (*Vaa pauses*) The situation has now reached the zenith. We cannot make this corporation a refuge for incompetents. I am now instructing you as Manager to pay off that boy before the close of today's work. Do that, please, forthwith!! Or have you been double-dealing? Good morning to you. (*Vaa exits*)

Voice: You can fool all the people sometime, but it is impossible to fool all the people all the time.

No-Balance (*diffidently*): Is this the end? (*No-Balance pauses*) Never! Never! Never! (*No*

Balance *confidently calls out to Bih who walks in*) Well boy, matters are very, very critical now. Who's to blame? I've been telling you from time immemorial to be very, very cautious with your work, or damnation would bless you. And here you are! Moreover, it was for your sake the Manager made some annoying remarks to me for which he did apologize afterwards. He suspects your being a kin and kith of mine, so needs my giving him more money than the amount you gave at first, though he feels ashamed to express it in words. (***No-Balance*** *pauses*) Yes. Do you know what I will do to help you? I'll extend my generosity to you, by carefully explaining matters to the Manager; on condition I have something on me to make me weighty before his eyes So, if you can afford, say, 10,000 francs or more, I promise, you are going to be re-employed and your bicycle allowance considered. In the absence of such, I'm afraid I just have to carry out the Manager's strict instructions by paying you off. That's that. (***Bih*** *takes in a deep breath and releases it.*)

Bih: Just one minute, sah. Now you ask for another monies? How about the monies I give...

No-Balance: No, no, no, no. Has the money you gave me not fetched you a job! It was meant that I comply with your dying wish of your becoming our Office boy, irrespective of your physique and qualification. And to that, I consented by ignoring your sluggishness to quote the Manager; and your inadequate qualification, evidenced by Jack's comments on your English. You know I am undertaking an uncalculated risk, now! This 10,000 francs is to help me win over the Manager to my side about your re-employment. Take note, I say re-employment and not, I repeat, not employment. (*He starts writing out Bih's termination letter*).

Bih: Well sah, I get no more monies to give you again, No-Balance. As for the monies I last squeeze into your dirty hands, eat it well. I do not want it again. But when it is in your stomach, it is God who will arrange it in a good or a bad place. Your papa who bore you saw in magic that you cannot never in your life balance when money and business are concerned; that is why he gave you the name "No-Balance." I no blame you. Even my pay money, chop am. Satan has blessed you. God for heaven is our Almighty. He knows my money and sees your tief and hears cry and suffer, of me.

No-Balance (*nervously*):   Hear your ear-drum-breaking English, O seeker of a job in my Office! You ungrateful idiot! You cause me risk my job! (***Bih*** *exits.* ***No-Balance*** *speaks confidently to himself.*) Tackle a situation with all amount of confidence and you find there is nothing before you to tackle. His 4,500 francs now goes to inflate my salary. After all, did Christ not sermon: the little will be taken from the poor and given to the rich?

Voice: Hear me you double-dealer; you have so far got what you want out of life, that i
money at any cost. Make use of the money, for in the end, honesty will prov
itself a better policy than vice.

No-Balance (*exits reciting*):   Day by day in every way, I am growing richer and
richer.

*The scene opens at the Police Station. Seated are **Constables Asongbu** and **Beagles**. A.S.P. **Edie** enters and both Constables stand up and salute. Then **Bih** enters very sorrowfully.*

Bih: Good morning sahs. My name is Bih and I have some case for Police. .

Beagles (*moves up to Edie*):   Sir, there is a boy here with a complaint. May I treat it?

Edie: Is it a complaint concerning money or what?

Bih: Sah. Yes sah! It is palaver for money palaver.

Edie (*nodding his head*):   All right. I'll handle it myself.
Beagles, please have we any case pending? Check up before I look into this.

> ***Beagles*** *goes through a voluminous book and shakes his head.*

Beagles: The last case was done with last night, sir.

Edie: Lucky chap. Can you speak a little English?

Bih: I can sah, but I am so vexed now that, I fear to spoil the English.

Edie: All right. Speak in pidgin English. (***Beagles*** *starts to write down the report.*)

Bih: Sah, one Chief Clerk advertisement for Office Boy and we application we plenty. As we application we plenty, he give we test for see di man weh pass we all. Bot before dis time, he tell me for backside say, make me I give him monies and he go give me the work. And me too, as I jam work pass mark, and I want work, bot I no get money, bot I see big man weh he dey like say he di sell work, I go turn, turn and borrow monies and give him two twice times. One times for he house and he office. We make test fine and na only me one pass. He take me for work correct, bot after two days only, he big masa sack me for work, for no palaver. I no tief, I no lie and I no curse di masa. The ting wonder me! So, sah, when I ask di man for give me back my monies, he only talk say make I give him another more monies before he go take me back for work. And me as I no get more monies again, I vex and cam report here for Charge Officer. (***Bih*** *weeps*)

Edie: Boy cool down. Now, what is the name of the Company?

Bih (*bringing out a piece of paper from his pocket and handing it over to Edie*): Sah, the name is very turf to call. So, I write it here on dis paper.

Edie: What, Vemsarbartreborp Corporation! That reputable Corporation! Therefore the Chief Clerk in question must be Mr. No-Balance.

Bih: Yes sah. Mr. No-Balance. Pure tief man! Tief man number one! Tief ma monie two twice times!

Beagles (*hushing him*): Don't make a scandal here!

Edie: Did you give the money before or after the test?

Bih: I say before the test and not behind.

Edie: How much money did you give him?

Bih: I give him monies two twice times. 10,000 francs in his Office and 16,000 francs in his house to befitul waf to keep.

Edie: How many of you did the test?

Bih: We three of us written it. One boy leave the test in the middle with vexation, the other boy, the man drive away. Only me alone passed the test.

Edie: This Chief Clerk must have done everything foul to see that the other candidate abandoned the test who, perhaps, gave him little or no money at all. Then, he passed this Bih as the successful candidate with the consciousness that he wouldn't have been able to cope with the others, judging by even his pidgin English.

However, unfortunately for this Chief Clerk, the Manager was keen enough to discover this boy's inefficiency early. Consequently, he then and there had to terminate his appointment before ever matters got worse. Ignorant of it all, the boy asked for the refund of his money forthwith... (*pauses, then conclusively*) This is a clear case of bribery. One of the most nation-killing, prevailing vices of the twentieth century. We cannot live to see it crop up in this our growing State. We must nip it in the bud.

Now, the Secret Branch takes up the challenge. (*He turns to Bih*) Boy, where does this Mr. No-Balance stay?

Bih: At Meno's Quarters.

Beagles and Asongbu: We know it sir. It is an airy point.

Edie: Okay boy, you can now go. We shall inform you through

Bih: … Statastas Office …

Edie: When you ought to be present in court. (*as Bih starts to leave an idea strikes* **Edie**) One minute. Bih is…

Bih: I no get clock, sah.

Asongbu: Shut up and listen.

Edie: Is this Mr. No-Balance married and living together with his wife?

Bih: He get sweet, fine, befitul waf for his house now, now.

Edie: Thank you, bye-bye and keep calm.

> (***Bih*** *exits. There is silence as* ***Edie*** *does some deep thinking. Then, he smiles as an idea dawns on him.*)

Edie: I've got it. Take a pen and a paper, Constable Asongbu. Write out a letter to Mrs. No-Balance as if you're a relative. Not as a sister or brother, for, we have no idea as to her having either but she must have a relative. Or she's a devil …

Asongbu (*cutting in*): Even devils have relatives.

Edie: O.K. In the letter, inform her of your being in a critical condition and need her presence without the least delay. Done and finished with that, (*smiles*) you will disguise yourself in the dress of a postman and deliver the letter to her in person. Impress on her the importance of the letter. You may even assist her in the packing if need be. And make sure she goes out of town before you return. (*He inhales deeply, pats his hair and exhales with a smile*) Do you know the next move Officers of Law and Order? As soon as she is away the persuasive tongue and radiant beauty of our Officer Maggie will be with this Mr. No-Balance to extract every substance out of him with a tape-recorder. No matter the short space of time, her records recommend her for this game. Officers, come what may, that's my line of action!

> *After writing and putting the letter in an envelope,* ***Asongbu*** *salutes and goes out.*

Edie: Beagles fetch us Officer Maggie.

***Beagles** goes out and returns accompanied by Officer Maggie.*

Maggie (*saluting*):   At you service, sir.

Edie (*motioning her to a seat opposite him*):   Officer Maggie, are you occupied?

Maggie: No sir. I am not occupied.

Edie: Now, Officer Maggie, the State once again needs one of your unbelievable miraculous and indispensable services. Here is a case of bribery. (*He allows her to go through the report; she reads and smiles*). As you can see, this case needs a first rate operator. I've weighed all the Officers of the Upper Secret Branch and found you the only one competent to carry out the operation. We need the best of your manoeuvres at this game. (*He produces a tape-recorder and hands it over to her*). Here is one of your apparatuses for the operation; a tape-recorder. You may be in need of it through circumstances. There's a note mentioned in the report. Try to fish it out. Exhibit 'A' for the Court. Any comments?

Maggie: The operation will be effected efficiently and within the calculated period as long as the operation is the only cure. And don't forget my watchword:
Three faces wears Officer Maggie when first sought: Confidence submissiveness, the investigation half wrought. The investigation over she seeks her fee. The devil looks less fearful than she (*She is about to go*).

Edie: Follow constable Asongbu. As soon as they set out for their journey, count one to thirty gradually, then take up your role. I wish you success in your cover operations.   (***Maggie*** *exits*) Well constable Beagles, keep me posted -- I'm off (***Edie*** *exits*)

The scene moves to Mr. No-Balance's sitting-room where he is with Mbarama, chatting away. Shortly, there comes a knock at the door and **Constable Asongbu** *enters, dressed as a postman.*

Asongbu: Good afternoon. Please, am I, at present, speaking to Mrs. No-Balance?

Mbarama: Yes. Mrs. No-Balance listens to you. There's Mr. No-Balance. (*Mr. No-Balance pretends to doze.*) Sorry, he's dozing away in the chair.

Asongbu: Don't worry. Here's a letter for you. It came by post and I'm commissioned by the postmaster to deliver it to you in person and urge you comply with the contents forthwith. He, the postmaster, received a phone call from the writer on the importance of the letter before it arrived. (*She tears open the envelope, unfolds the letter with quivering fingers, goes through it and her eyes goggle. She wakes up No-Balance*).

Mbarama: Darling dear, a letter from my aunt at Lobito Bay, expressing her critical condition and her dying need for my immediate presence. I must be leaving right away. (*To Asongbu*) Please, postman, I'll need your company to the bus stop.
(*She starts packing. She comes across the piece of paper on which she wrote the names of the applicants and the gifts they offered. She puts the piece of paper away in her purse and places the purse on the chair.*)

No-Balance: Tomato, when do I expect you back?

Mbarama: As soon as there's a bit of improvement in her health, I'll come back.

No-Balance: You need 3,000 francs to travel with?

Mbarama (*frowns, and ignores Asongbu's presence*): What have you done with the money given you only yesterday that you give me only 3.000 francs. Don't give me cause to...

No-Balance (*winks at her*): There's money. Take 6,000 francs. I expect you back in nine days. (*She kisses him, bids him farewell and she's in such haste that she forgets her purse on the chair. Mbarama and Asongbu both exit.*)

No-Balance: Oh me! For how long will I remain alone! I pray not for long. (*There's a pause and No-Balance relaxes. Then there is a knock at the door and a lady enters. It is Maggie carrying a suitcase*).

27

Maggie: Good morning, Sir. Am I, at this moment, speaking to Mr. No-Balance?

No-Balance: You are. Can I help you? Sit down, Miss or Madam. (*She sits down cautiously and throws a cursory glance around the room*).

Maggie: My name is Maggie. I am a second year student in the University of Infliction and am pursuing Criminology.

No-Balance (*Shaking hands with her*): I'm more than delighted to meet you, Miss Maggie. It's the highest time we had criminologists, as vices of untold nature are creeping into this our young State. I hope you'll cut a nice figure?

Maggie: Let's hope so. Well, I received a letter from my niece, Mbarama informing me of her impending marriage to you. We're out for three days field work, so I decided to pass the night here and to move up to our next station tomorrow. By the way, where's Mbarama?

(*He is attracted by her beauty, and betrays it by telling a lie.*)

No-Balance: You might have passed her on the way as she goes to see a sister some three miles away from here. She, however, has to be back this evening or at latest, very early tomorrow morning. All the same, make yourself at home.

Maggie (*pretentiously*): My flesh is happy to stay, but my soul is unwilling. Never mind, it's still my home. Please, may I get some drinking water?

No-Balance: No, I'll get some beer in place of water.

Maggie: Sorry. I take only whisky.

No-Balance: From water to spirit, you'll have it.

(***No-Balance*** *goes out for the whisky.* ***Maggie*** *quickly searches through her bookshelf, moves about the room searchingly, then, sits down disappointedly. She picks up the purse lying on the chair, opens it and finds the piece of paper put there by Mbarama. She goes through it, smiles then hides it away in her brassiere. Then she pretends to doze as No-Balance enters.*)

No-Balance: I'm sorry to have left you alone.

Maggie: No harm done. I only felt a bit drowsy; but will now clear it with the

28

whisky. (*She serves herself and makes a curt toast*). Whatever sky is above you, let it fall on you, Mr. No-Balance.

No-Balance (*responding*): May the Gods grant your wishes, O earthly angel. (*Short silence*) Maggie, I hope I'll not be hurting your feelings if I put this to you?

Maggie: Why must I be hurt in a conversation with my nephew-in-law?

No-Balance: Not as yet, I'm not yet married and you may be the one. (*Both laugh*) Anyway, we just keep the ball rolling. Maggie, how do you go about love affairs in the University? I mean, is there anybody at present occupying your heart without rent? (*Silence as Maggie pretends to battle with shyness*)

Maggie: I'll answer in plain simplicity. We students of criminology, by law of our profession, have our hearts occupied without rent only for a period, and such a period could be, for instance, now. (*She gives him a sidelong glance and sips her drink. This brightens No-Balance's hopes as he scratches his head, sips his drink and lunches his appeal*).

No-Balance: Can you not make this one of such rare periods? It's a matter of pressing your lips against mine and then, allowing some currents to run down my nerves, no, yours too. What say you? (*Silence as he watches her*) But if you don't like it, just take it easy.

Maggie: Won't I be back-stabbing my niece?

No-Balance: Be your age, Maggie. How can she have an idea of it? Is she a goddess? And even if she does and tends to make a fuss over it, I'll simply give her the boot and take you in her place.

Maggie: Remember nothing ever happens without an onlooker. (*Pauses*) That we fear death, shouldn't make us deny ourselves sleep.

No-Balance (*seizing her by the hand*): Do you want to kill me right away! All will be lifeless until you change your mind.

Maggie: An itching around my lips,
To me renders unease;
Devotedly press your pursed lips,
Against mine, return my ease

(*She sits still. Then **No-Balance** gradually moves his lips to hers and they kiss.*

29

She pulls away from him.)

No-Balance: Maggie, when you make yourself agreeable, you're not only agreeable .. Please, one more of such currents through my nerves. I've lost my brains over you. (*He goes out to make sure nobody is around*) Darling, have no fear. Everything is under control. (*He moves closer to her for more kisses but she stops him*).

Maggie: Wait a minute. Your liveliness has just reminded me of one of the unforgettable incidents in my romantic life. (*She pretends to weep*) There's a boy to whom I actually allowed my heart without a franc. My lips were his to kiss; my body, his to caress, my companion whenever he demanded, but dear me, he so shocked me one day that I almost committed murder! The heavens, however, prevented it and the boy gave me the slip. I pray he falls into the hands of any of my relatives so that I stand by and admire the tortures being inflicted upon him.

No-Balance: By the way, what's his name?

Maggie: Bih.

No-Balance: There you are! That's the very boy I employed for three consecutive days. Just these last three days. If you had only called here earlier!

Maggie: What! Bih summoned assistance from you? Please, do you still have the whole scene fresh in your memory?

No-Balance: I can still imagine myself and the kid standing and my spinning him around.

Maggie: Do. I'll therefore have your memoir of it. I like to have a catalogue of that chap's misfortune, just for enjoyment purposes.

(*She gives No-Balance a kiss which maddens him the more She then opens her suitcase, puts the tape-recorder on undetected, and gets out a piece of paper on which she stealthily takes down the incident as No-Balance narrates it. No-Balance, now fully intoxicated by the drink and Maggie's kisses, reveals the whole incident to her.*)

No-Balance: This Bih came to me for employment as an office boy for which I advertised. I'm sure you're aware of the fact that I'm the Chief Clerk of our corporation and the prospective manager.
Well, I saw this chap to be one who has been battling with life and

30

needed some help. So, I decided to help him. Three of them applied for the advertised post. Among them Bih was the dullest. All the same, as I'm generous, as you already know and had also decided to help him, I assured him of the job provided he gave me some money. (*Sips his drink*) He responded so lively, giving me 10,000 francs and 16,000 francs on two different occasions. With such backing, I had to favour him in the test, irrespective of his poor performances. He was employed alright, but was inefficient; and this inefficiency didn't pass unnoticed by my Manager. (*Pauses*)

In spite of my tactful interventions, the Manager overruled me one unfortunate morning and gave him the boot. Again, still with my same generosity, I asked him to give me 10,000 francs more in order to get himself re-employed. Then and there he went off in a huff and has not returned. (*He fills his glass and sips it*)

I expect him back one day; then, I'll teach him to be angry with the right person, in the right degree for the right purpose in the right way and at the right time. That's how I spun him. Am I not wonderful? (*Staggers towards Maggie who avoids him*)

Maggie: You really spun him a tale. I wish I were here only yesterday! Hope we shall go out for a walk this evening? However, let me inform my colleagues that I'll be passing the night here. (*She is about to go away, then pretends to recollect*) Do give me your full name and address of the house so that they will know where to collect me tomorrow morning. (*She discreetly takes the piece of paper on which she has written the report as narrated by No-Balance for him to sign without knowing. He hesitates, then writes out his name and address, and adds his signature*).

No-Balance: That's a unique signature! (*Maggie gives him a short kiss and goes off with the piece of paper and the tape-recorder*).

Voice: Mr. No-Balance, Woe betide you!

No Balance: I am going to get ready for our stroll tonight. (*He goes out and returns shortly ready for the evening outing with Maggie. He looks a bit worried when Maggie enters*).

Maggie: It's a pity. I had to keep you on cold feet. Hope you're not hurt?

No-Balance (*moving up to her*): How can I be hurt by beauty keeping me indoors!

(*He's about to kiss her when **Constable Beagles** barges in.*)

31

Maggie (*feigning surprise*): A policeman! (*She runs off and hides in a corner*).

No-Balance (*going red*): What right have you to walk into my house unannounced?

Beagles (*stands arms akimbo*): Finish with your love affairs, then, I'll carry out m~~y~~ mission.

No-Balance: I'm not a culprit, Get out!

Beagles (*calmly identifying himself*): I'm Constable Beagles and you're Mr. No-Balance. With the powers invested in me, I arrest you in the name of the People, for encouraging and executing bribery, which according to a Presidentia~~l~~ decree, is an act against the State. Being a matter now between you and the People, you'll speak yourself to conviction or acquittal before famous Justice Snaps

(*No-Balance is handcuffed by Beagles. Shortly thereafter, Maggie reenter~~s~~ shedding crocodile tears.*)

Maggie: Constable, how cruel of you to treat my husband thus! Do have pity on him.

No-Balance: Do, Constable, allow me some private minutes with my wife. (*Beagles goes out*) Maggie, why do you weep? My brain is indefatigable. I've a root in this matter, and now that another akin to it is touching it, it must also become the root of the matter. Get a 5,000 francs note from my hip pocket. (*She does so*) Copy out the number and then, offer the money to the police man. Insist on his taking it. This done and finished with, shut the doors and windows and follow me to court where you'll see me in my last role of this drama. As soon as he finishes prosecuting me, I also will take to prosecuting him. But remember, you are my principal and only witness.

Maggie: Didn't I tell you of the unwillingness of my soul to be here? If it happens that matters prove to be tragic, that journalist may label it as "The Tragedy of Mr. No-Balance," but God forbid it, let me speak to you a bit. There is no use having a defence counsel; only as you're in the dock, I'll be in court, speak with all confidence, I'll be praying to all th~~e~~ Gods for you.

(*No-Balance goes out as Beagles re-enters.*)

32

Maggie (*whispering*):   He gave me, 5,000 francs to bribe you with: then he'll accuse you of having solicited in court and call me to witness. I tell you he's a devil of a man!

*(**Maggie** and **Beagles** go off.)*

The High Court, which is the theatre itself, is packed full and seen conspicuously are Bih, Jack, Maggie, Ernest and No-Balance. The sound of the engine of a car which drives into the Court premises is heard and this draws the attention of Ernest and No-Balance. They both fall into a conversation.

Ernest: No-Balance have you seen the car driven by Justice Snaps?

No-Balance: It's a Volvo! The most pleasurable, and of all, the most safe car I've ever seen and heard of.

Ernest: Who sells it?

No-Balance: Niba Automobile Company in Dibanda. Ernest, I very much long to have one.

Ernest: In this your present state?

No-Balance: Never mind. It will all be over soon.

Ernest (*hushing him to be silent*):   The Judge is coming in now.

> (*There's the sound of the gavel. All stand up as **Snap**s enters and all sit after he does. **Law**, the Court Clerk, remains standing.*)

Snaps: Proceed.

Law: Case number one and only one is: The People versus Zacharias Kongmelina No-Balance. No-Balance, into the dock you go. (***No- Balance** enters the docket and **Law** reads the charge*)
You, Zacharias Kongmelina No-Balance, were on the twenty-fourth day of the first month in the year of our Lord, one thousand nine hundred and sixty, investigated and found out to have encouraged and executed bribery with such an incredible degree of malice that the other party had nothing to go on for the rest of his life. And this, according to Presidential Decree Number 147, Chapter 37, line 37 of 1957, is an act against the State. Are you guilty or not guilty?

No-Balance: I'm not guilty your Lordship.

Law: He pleads "not guilty" your Lordship. (***No-Balance** enters the prosecuting box and he swears an oath on the Bible*).

No-Balance: I swear to the Almighty God, that the evidence I shall give in court shall be the truth, the whole truth, and nothing but the truth.

Snaps: Mr. No-Balance, have you any counsel?

No-Balance: I'm defending myself.

Snaps: Before the proceeding continues, I have to warn all persons concerned in this case that if you have the eloquence of speaking much and saying nothing, you should endeavour at all cost to avoid it in this case; otherwise, you'll be treated severely in the course of the case. Let all the witnesses in this case, keep out of court and earshot.

(The witnesses go out.)

Pat: You are Zacharias Kongmelina No-Balance?

No-Balance: Of course, I am he.

Pat: Chief Clerk of Vemsarbatreborp Corporation?

No-Balance: Still the very I, as well as a Prospective Manager.

Pat: Now, have you once come across anybody who goes by the name Bih?

No-Balance: Bih, Bih, Bih. Definitely! I know one little brat by that name.

Pat: Give the court a full account of your connections with this Bih.

No-Balance: Bih is a small boy who was sometime employed in my office as an office boy, but was later dismissed for inefficiency although …

Pat: What's the "although?"

No-Balance: No, a slip of the tongue.

Snaps: Look here Mr. No-Balance, you're a learned man and not supposed to be making incomplete sentences on such a serious occasion in the guise of a slip of the tongue. Now, complete your sentence.

No-Balance (*angrily*): Although I intended helping him, I had second thoughts and dropped the idea.

35

Snaps: Mr. No-Balance. I have to warn you again! You're not to get into temper in my court.

                (**Pat**, *the prosecutor, stands up.*)

Pat: If you were to help him, what sort of help could you have rendered him?

No-Balance: That would have been a matter between him and whosoever dismisse₄ him.

Pat: So before all this, you never entered into any business terms with Bih?

No-Balance: Could you yourself have dealings with such a brat?

Snaps: Zacharias Kongmelina No-Balance, you are not to answer th₄ prosecution's question by a question.

Pat: Your Lordship, may I have Bih in the dock?

Snaps: If that is necessary.

Law: Bih, into the dock, please.

(**Bih** *enters and takes the oath.*)

Bih: I swear to the Almighty God, that all that I shall say here in court sha₄ be the truth, the whole truth, and nothing but the truth.

Pet: You're Bih?

Bih: Na me sah.

Pat: You sometimes worked for Vemsabatreborp Corporation as an office boy?

Bih: Yes sah, for only two days, sah.

Pet: Do you know that gentleman? *(pointing at No-Balance)*

Bih: Yes sah! He was my big man for work. He got monies from me and …

Snaps *(cutting in)*: Answer the question accordingly.

36

Bih: Yes sah.

Pat: Now, tell the court all your connections with that gentleman.

Bih: Sah, he advertisement for office boy in his office. Three of us written for the post. One of the boy by name em … em … em …

Jack: I'm here, I'm Jack.

Snaps: Boy, one more of such interruption and you'll be charged with contempt of court.

Bih: Yes, Jack went away in the middle of the test with vexation, while the other boy the man drove him away. So it was I that passed the test. But before this, he told me at the backside that I must give him money and he will give me the job. So as I jam work pass mark, and I want for work bot I no get money, bot I see some big man weh he dey like he want to seel work, I turn, turn and borrow money and gave him two twice times, 10,000 francs and 16,000 francs in his office and his house.

I entered work correct, and after two days only, his Manager sacked me for no reason. I no tief, I no lie, I no curse any man. It was wonder to me! So, when I asked this man for give back my monies, he told me to give him more monies before the Manager is taking me back to work. Me too, as I no get more monies, I cam report for police. (*Turns to No-Balance*) Sah, am I lie?

Snaps: Don't be rude or I will discipline you, Have you any question to ask him, Mr. No-Balance?

No-Balance: Boy, was anybody present when you were giving me the money?

Bih: We were only we two only.

No-Balance: Can you prove that I asked for the money before you gave me?

Bih: Judge is to dig it today here in court.

No-Balance: Didn't you fare well in the test?

Bih: Was I going on journey to farewell?

Law (*cutting in*): Did you not do well in the test?

Bih: That is how the man is bringing confusion everywhere! I cannot know if I d well in the test because the other boys do not do the test, only me alone.

No-Balance: That's all, your Lordship.

Pat: Bih, did you give him the money before or after the test?

Bih: I gave him the money two twice times before the test and not behind it.

Pat: What caused Jack to go away in anger?

Bih: Well sah, I do not have any senses in that but the boy said that there was som foul in the test. As for me, I saw no foul in the office.

Pat: What caused him to send away the other boy?

Bih: All that I saw was that after the man talked witt the boy some cunny talk, h became vex and was looking for the telephone to phone a policeman. The bo beg and ran away calling God.

Pat: What do you mean by "some cunny talk?"

Bih: That is, talk that I no fit make its head or its tail.

Pat: That's all, your Lordship. (*There is silence as* **Bih** *steps down*) Mr. No-Balance, hav you once in your life signed your name under duress?

No-Balance: Never in the history of my thirty-one years stay on earth.

Pat: How many signatures have you?

No-Balance: As a growing V.I.P. I have two signatures; one for official matters an the other for non-official matters.

Pat: Carefully write out your non-official signature here as you would on occasion. (*A paper is provided for No-Balance on which he writes out his signature.* **Pat** *compares it wit the one on the report and passes it on to* **Snaps** *who compares it also and shakes his head Do write it out clearly. (***No-Balance** *does so again and the same procedure takes pla again*)

Snaps: Mr. No-Balance, my professional training induces me to disbelieve you; m instinct tells me you're between and betwixt. Nonetheless, have you an witnesses?

No-Balance: Your Lordship, I have two witnesses; Messrs Zaacs and Noah.

Law: Zaacs, take your place in the dock.

(*Zaacs* *enters the dock and takes the oath.*)

Zaacs: I swear to the Almighty God that the evidence I shall give in court shall be the truth, the whole truth, and nothing but 1 truth.

Pat: You are?

Zaacs: Zaacs.

Pat: You're witness to whom?

Zaacs: To the defendant.

Pat: You're what to him?

Zaacs: I'm his friend.

Pat: What's your occupation?

Zaacs: I'm a businessman.

Pat: Now tell the court all that you know about this case.

Zaacs: One morning, on a date I have forgotten, I went to Mr. No-Balance's house to tell him about the car he intended buying. On my entering the house, I saw this Bih who was actually on his knees before Mr. No-Balance praying him, No-Balance, to take something which he had parcelled in a handkerchief. Mr. No-Balance was not prepared to receive it, for I heard him asking the boy to leave his house or he was going to phone for the police. All the while the boy wasn't aware of my entry and presence. But as soon as he became aware he guiltily stood up, and was about to bolt away when I stepped in his way. He frowned so hard that I let him go away. Later on, however, my friend revealed to me that the boy was offering him some gifts, perhaps in cash or kind in order to be favoured in the recruiting test for an office boy advertised by Mr. No-Balance's office. On hearing this, I advised No-Balance not to dare it; even to see to it that he failed in the test. That over, I went about my business.

The next morning, when I went to No-Balance's office on somethin confidential, I met three boys in his office including this Bih taking a test. An believe you me, your Lordship, this Bih proved so efficient in the test that m friend had no other alternative than to engage him and make him start wor there and then.

Two days afterwards, No-Balance informed me of Bih's dismissal by th Manager because of his sluggishness. I only smiled, made the sign of the cross a a faithful follower of Christ and went about my business.

I was surprised when I heard last night that Mr. No-Balance had been arreste and was to be arraigned before the High Court; also that he had asked me t come as his witness. That's all I know about the case.

Pat: Were you with Mr. No-Balance from the moment Bih bolted out of his house u to the following day that the test took place in the office?

Zaacs: I wasn't with him all day.

Pat: Do you know that after you left No-Balance Bih returned to offer him the parce which he did at last receive?

Zaacs: I didn't know that and even if Bih returned I am as sure as ever that No-Balanc didn't accept the parcel.

Pat: Were you aware of the fact that the other two candidates abandoned the te before ever it came to an end?

Zaacs: I went to the toilet where I spent over twenty minutes as I am suffering from chronic dysentery. On my return, my friend showed me only Bih's marks as th successful candidate. So, I simply concluded within me that the others hasti disappeared from the scene as defeated men.

Pat: Your Lordship that's all. The next witness. Noah.

Law: Noah, take your place in the dock.

(**Noah** *enters the dock and takes the oath.*)

Noah: I swear by the Almighty God, that the evidence I shall give here in this cou shall be the truth, the whole truth, and nothing but the truth.

Pat: Your name?

40

Noah: Noah.

Pat: You're witness to whom?

Noah: The defendant.

Pat: You're what to him?

Noah: Nothing but a sympathizer

Pat: Your occupation?

Noah: Farmer.

Pat: Go ahead with all your facts about this case.

Noah: On a certain evening, on a certain day this month, I was preparing to have a bath after a day's work, when this my little cousin, Bih, came in crying. On my asking him the cause of it, he told me of his having been dismissed from his job for no reason. I asked him if he was sure he had committed no offence. He assured me of his innocence, but revealed that he wasn't liked by the Chief Clerk, and was sure it was he who recommended his dismissal. And he went further to say that he was going to undo the Chief Clerk. I however, advised him to be calm and not to be worried over it and that I was going to investigate it all.
He became angry and was about to go away when I saw Mr. No-Balance passing by my house. "What luck," I exclaimed. When I called to him to know all that had passed between the Manager and Bih, Bih went away in a huff, but No-Balance was patient enough to explain all to me. I was planning to call both of them today to settle the matter when I heard that No-Balance had been arrested for receiving money from Bih. That's all.

Pat: How does Mr. No-Balance's receiving money from Bih connect with his dismissal that you decided to come as a sympathizer?

Noah: Because Bih told me that he was going to undo Mr. No-Balance. So I just felt that he must have devised a means to affect that as vengeance.

Pat: Noah, what's your tribe?

Noah: I come from Bangwi.

Pat: That's all your Lordship. Bih, once more into the dock. (*Bih enters the dock*)

41

Law: Do you know you're still on oath?

Bih: Yes sah.

Pat: Bih, do you know the gentleman who just left the dock now called Noah?

Bih: I know only Noah and his ark. I never knew there is somebody too with th
name Noah, only here in court.

Pat: What's your tribe?

Bih: I come from Bafaw pure, Mama and Papa. (*Bih steps down.*)

Pat: That's all your Lordship. Re-examination of the defendant if it pleases the court.

Snaps: If it is necessary.

Pat: Mr. No-Balance, can you recognize your voice if you hear it anywhere and a
anytime?

No-Balance: If it's possible, I surely can and will.

Pat: Now listen to this. (*He produces the tape-recorder which Maggie used during th*
investigation, puts it on, and **No-Balance's** *voice is heard as he narrates the incident betwee*
himself and Bih to Maggie. The narrative ends.) Mr. No-Balance, can you nov
recognize that voice? (*There is no response. No-Balance is completely tongue-tied and gaze*
stupidly into space).
Your Lordship, there is the point of a Bangwi man claiming a Bafaw chap as
relative, a cousin for that matter, but no relationship whatsoever was proven
here is the voice of a man who can no longer say whether it's his voice or no
despite all the boasts in the speech concerning the theme of this case -- bribery
his speechlessness and stupid gaze reveals surprise and guilt. Come what may
the case unfolds itself. I beg to take my seat.

> (*There is dead silence.*)

Snaps: Mr. Zacharias Kongmelina No-Balance, the unusual proceedings in this court ar
confessions of my being frightfully in great sympathy with you, in that I'll b
harming you unjustly to deprive you of your future prospects in you
Corporation. All the same, I see it will be folly of me to exhibit mercy when you
respect for the simple truth is conspicuously minus at every step, though yo

have yet to make your final plea.

You had to do everything within, and even without your office to see that the other boys abandoned the test, who perhaps gave you no money at all. And you took Bih as the successful candidate because of the heavy purse he used in weighing down the scales of justice. But in reality, this Bih isn't fit to be an office boy, judging from his English.

Mr. No-Balance, you have been carefully weighed in the scales of justice, and found as light as paper.

Your betrayal has been as artful as your masterful plan for bribery.

Depriving you of your rights according to the Presidential Decree will be the only cure of the liberty you have misused.

Have you anything to say before I pass judgment?

(No-Balance composes himself, says nothing, and hangs his head apparently in shame. There is dead silence as Snaps pores through many voluminous books.)

Snaps: How old are you?

No-Balance (*with meekness*): Thirty-one years of age.

Snaps: No-Balance, youthful age always moves me to less severity. Your youth and meekness impels me to invoke every possible branch of the law to your aid. So, by Section 333 of the Infliction code and by Article 110, 11, Chapter 0,002,023, Line 222, 121 of (Motale and Balla), I discharge you on the grounds of your pleadings. This court adjourns for five minutes.

Law: As your Lordship wishes it.

(Court stands up as Snaps goes out. Everybody is surprised at the judgment and Beagles approaches No-Balance.)

Beagles (*arresting No-Balance*): Mr. No-Balance, I arrest you for attempting to impede the course of justice by offering money to a policeman executing his duties. You now have to face Justice Snaps right away before ever you become wiser.

(There is consternation as No-Balance is marched back into Court; order is restored and Justice Snaps re-enters and sits down.)

Law: The next case is again: The People versus Zacharias Kongmelina No-Balance. No-Balance, take your place in the dock! (*No- Balance re-enters the dock and Law reads out the charge*) You Zacharias Kongmelina No-Balance on Friday afternoon of this very month at your residence, offered money to a Law Officer executing his duties with an eye to corrupting him and then influencing the law from taking its just course and this according to section 939 of the Infliction Code is an ac against the State. Are you guilty or not guilty?

No-Balance (*proudly*): Guilty with reasons ...

Snaps: Remember this is quite a fresh case outside the previous one. Now what are you reasons?

No-Balance: A certain police officer came to arrest me on a case of my receivin bribe of which I've just been discharged. He demanded my offering him som money and he would release me and then strike out the case from the polic records. I saw the dishonesty of the officer in executing his duties an irrespective of my being the alleged culprit, I decided to bring him to book. O this score, I secretly commissioned my sister-in-law, a student in the Universit of Infliction, who, luckily was doing her practical work and spending the tim with me, to copy out the number of a 5,000 francs note, and then offer th money to the officer. This, I planned to expose in court during the course of m case. As I didn't lose the case, I however, decided to give up the pursui Nonetheless my sister-in-law is still around whom I have as my principal witnes She is Maggie.

Snaps: Put Maggie in the dock.

(**Maggie** *enters the dock and takes the oath.*)

Maggie: I swear to the Almighty God, that the evidence I shall give here in cour shall be the truth, the whole truth, and nothing but the truth.
My name is Maggie. I am speaking for the accused. I'm an officer of th Upper Secret Branch.

No-Balance: You are what, Maggie?

Law: Keep quiet and wait for your turn.

No-Balance (*dejected*): My sister-in-law is bought over! She's charmed over! She melted over! Maggie, you're gone over.

Snaps: Shut up else you will further be charged with contempt of Court. Office Maggie, proceed.

Maggie: I investigated the foregone case. At the end, a police officer came fo

44

the arrest. No-Balance was confused when the officer showed up. Of his own accord, and without a demand from the officer hatched a plan to incriminate the officer. He would offer him 5,000 francs then later on accuse him of demanding bribe using the number of the note I had copied out with me as a witness. Unfortunately, he prepared two knots to knot up his one miserable, satanic head!

(**Maggie** *has hardly finished as No-Balance collapses shouting.*)

No-Balance: Destiny destines all. I am finished! The Law, pardon me! Pardon!

(*Silence as Snaps writes*)

Snaps: We are most in danger when we think ourselves secure; most secure when we feel ourselves to be most in danger. This is my summary of this case. With the powers invested upon me by Section 999 of the Infliction Code in dealing with such dramatic cases, and with the evidence before me, and the accused's acceptance of his guilt, I sentence Zacharias Kongmelina No-Balance to seven years imprisonment with very hard labour.
Take him away. This court stands adjourned for the day.

(*A Police officer puts* **No-Balance** *on his feet. He looks round to find that almost everybody has gone away, except the police officers and the court officials. He then exclaims.*)

No-Balance: I slept and dreamt that life was beauty. I woke and found that life is duty.

(*A manacled* **No-Balance** *is escorted out by the Police*)

THE END

This play has some good situations, reflecting aspects of life in the growing towns o
Africa. Petty bribery so often becomes an unsuccessful attempt by the small man to mak
some quick money out of an even smaller man. He only imitates the bribery practiced b
the big man who frequently seems to get away with it. "It is our way of life ..." -- bu
only for some.

There are two points to make about this play: firstly, Mr. Musinga does not despis
the characters he creates, he observes them closely and builds up complex relationship
secondly, he uses English to capture the tone and style of urban life exceedingly well, an
he creates a language for the African theatre which is full of vivid expression.

If you were producing this play, therefore, you would want to keep the dialogue a
more than just a basis for your own improvisation. Your actors may well have the abilit
to achieve a very funny and sophisticated urban style - but the trouble with improvisatio
is that it can so easily become excessive: your actors, the very ones who are mos
competent and comic, can so easily fall into a parody of the characters. Many of you
audience will feel uncomfortable if you mock the people Musinga has written about i
this play.

When you first tell an actor to make up his own dialogue as he goes along, h
worries that he won't have enough to say. Once he has gained confidence, he usuall
finds he has too much to say, The art of improvisation lies in understanding you
audience's responses very well. A line or a gesture may make an audience laugh and cla
in appreciation of an accurate imitation of life; but if you keep on doing it their laughte
soon stops. One of the achievements of Mr. Musinga's dialogue is the way in which h
exercises restraint. A person whose mind still remains colonized will accept a parody c
himself as being a 'normal" representation of himself, A sincere writer, or actor c
producer, has a political responsibility to help his audience to see every member of th
community as both an individual in his own right and a product of the forces of societ
operating upon him.

Mr. Musinga succeeds because he appears to be writing from within society. He ha
not marked off his characters from the rest of us. No-Balance and the rest as us
whoever we are or however grand we think we may be. This gift for creating commo
humanity In the midst of social change is a rare thing for actors and directors who ar
looking for a genuinely contemporary drama.

However, I should not like to suggest that the text is completely inflexible. There ar
changes which can be made and indeed changes, which ought to be made -- in order t
make the play suitable for both your theatre company and your potential audiences.
have itemized these as follows:

1. The C.I.D. detectives could make reference to actual cases solved by the police know
to members of the community before whom you will be performing. The character c
Edie, the A.S.P. (Security) man, should be modelled on actuality rather than the strip
comic image of the hero-cop of those magazines sold on every newsstand up and dow

46

Africa.

2. If you have only a small group of actors, the following characters can be doubled up and played by the same actor:

Vaa, Beagles and Judge Snaps;

Jack, Edie, Law;

Muke and Maggie;

Wawah, Asongbu, Zaacs and Noah.

No-Balance

Mbarama   (these cannot be doubled)

Bih ..

3. Victor Musinga suggests one way in which the Voice of No-Balance's conscience might be handled, which is as follows: for Voice to seem to come from within No-Balance, let the speeches of voice be taped on a pocket-sized tape-recorder and a carefully calculated space be left between one speech and another. The tape-recorder can be carried in the breast-pocket of the actor playing the part of No- Balance. Now, whenever it's the turn of Voice to be heard, all that No-Balance has to do is switch on the tape by pressing the button (unnoticed by the audience) and then perform the appropriate actions. After which, the tape can be switched off, still unnoticed, until the next time when Voice has to come in. Another way would be to place someone out of sight (up a tree, if you are performing outside, or behind the wings of the stage if you are inside) with a loud-hailer -- a portable megaphone which works off batteries.

4. Do not fuss about complicated scenery and you won't become involved in difficult scene changes. Obviously you must have items of furniture and objects which are mentioned in the text as being used by the characters. A free-standing door-frame with a door which opens and closes will quickly convince your audience that there are rooms with walls between. Indicate the different places by rearranging the furniture and hanging up a large banner which indicates where the scene is taking place).

5. I personally feel that the final court-room scene is too long. It is obviously necessary to have No-Balance tried twice, but extensive cuts could be made in Zaac's speeches, Snaps' long speech and No-Balance's plea for clemency. The whole scene has a zany quality to it anyway, and should be acted very fast (normally you would think of a High Court as sedate, ponderous and serious -- but if you play the scene this way you will bore your audience to death). An absolute minimum of time should be taken administering the oath and getting people on and off stage. Victor Musinga has obviously been conscious of the need for speed because he has written this scene in such a way that you can act it very fast indeed.

Michael ETHERTON